Adult Coloring Book Birds & Flowers

Relaxation

101 Images Beginner to Advanced

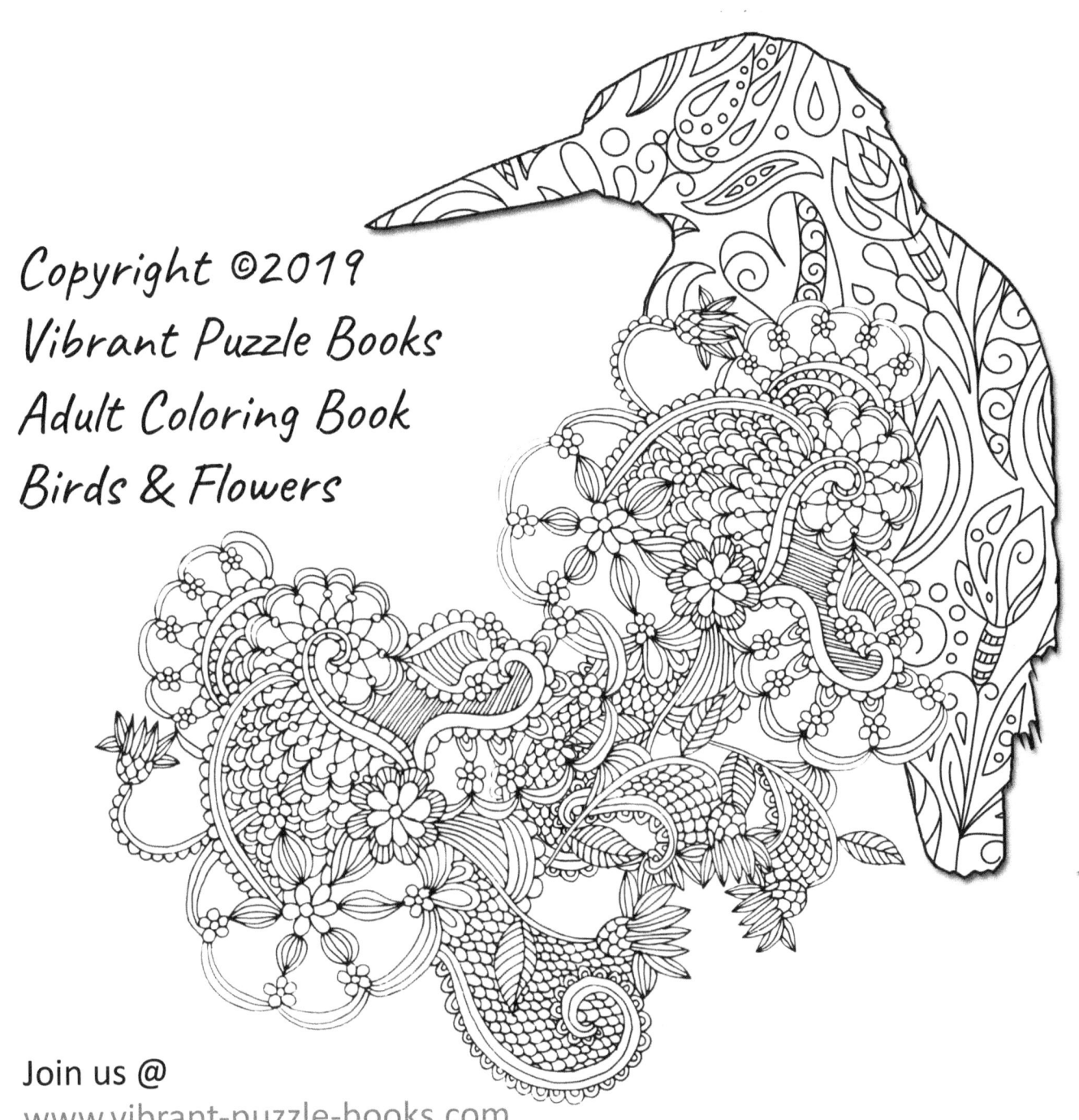

Copyright ©2019
Vibrant Puzzle Books
Adult Coloring Book
Birds & Flowers

Join us @
www.vibrant-puzzle-books.com
Facebook: VibrantBooks
Twitter: BooksVibrant
Pinterest: Vibrant_Books
Instagram: adult_coloring_puzzle_books

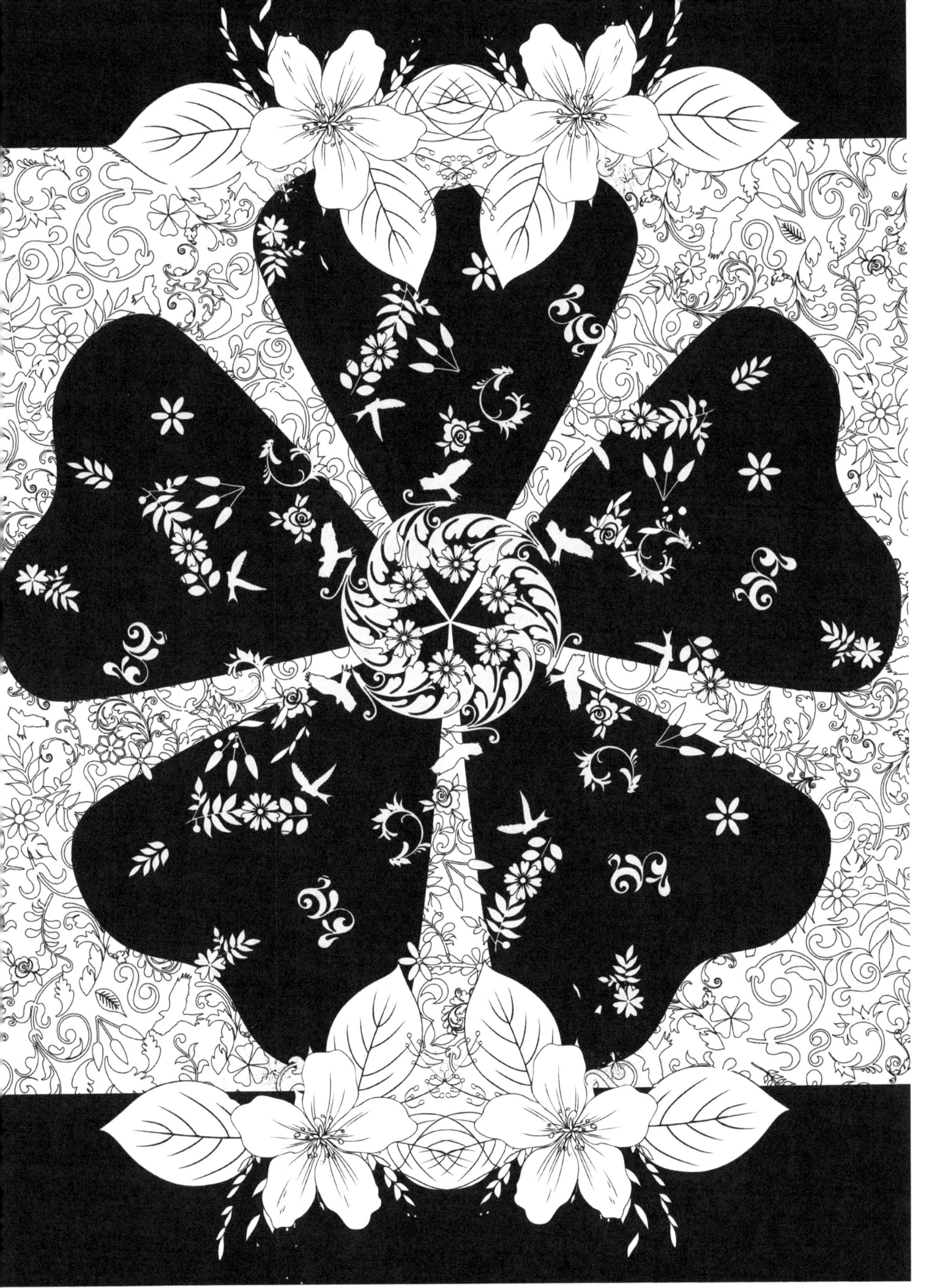

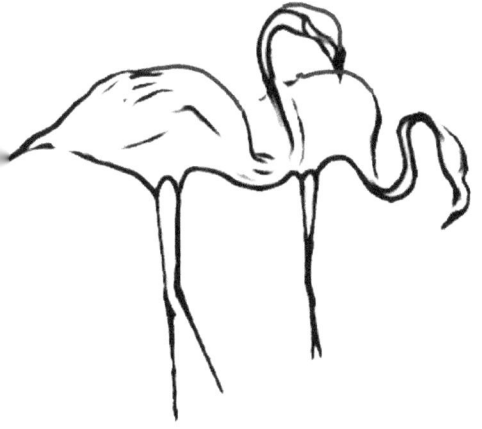

www.vibrant-puzzle-books.com
Join us @
Facebook: VibrantBooks
Twitter: BooksVibrant
Pinterest: Vibrant_Books
Instagram: adult_coloring_puzzle_books

www.ingramcontent.com/pod-product-compliance
Lightning Source LLC
Chambersburg PA
CBHW081443070526
44586CB00019B/2216